No Direction But Home

Sarah Whiteley

for my family -
home is wherever you are

and for S. -
who doesn't know he still inspires

CONTENTS

the memory of place

my heart has plucked
a chord from the air
and this is the sound
of my wonderment

nights like this
the skin remembers
that it was once
of the sea

and is drawn up
by the moon's
hushful gravity

it is possible
I think, to know
the sound of a place
and love it

so that it here
creates a cavity
where it might
rest in echoes

and rise at night
to awaken us,
to make us think
that we though here,
are wandering
back there

summer reflection

sitting on the edge of the dock,
rough wood bleached gray
by wind and winters past
bites into pale thighs
while toes tease the water
into swirls of cool reflection

we used to lay here on our bellies
our heads over the edge,
watching the bluegills as they
swam out from the shadows
between the posts

from here I can count
the bright flash of birch
emerging from the pines
sixteen lines of white that rise
and lean over the rocks
that mark the shore

I've found that if you stand like that,
leaning far out over the water,
there's a pull between the trees
that rise behind and the twists of sky
that scud along the water's surface

and the quiet cool calls to you
from beneath, a beckoning that insists
upon precarious angles and it's a small
thing to lose yourself completely
or at the very least your balance

it's a fall we didn't much mind
if it meant a sudden release
from an afternoon heat
that stuck to the skin
like plum juice to fingers

those stones we skipped years ago
are somewhere under there, flat and gray
between the surface and the sand,
and for all we know the fish
were appreciative of the change in décor

sitting here now, it seems I've
missed somehow the moment
our summers passed
into not enough time

and yet the shapes of turtles
still rise at dusk, dark heads
breaking the surface,
jumping distance from this old dock

in this place the loons
have always called the night down
in the darkening hours,
when the trees have turned
into their own tall shadows

and long after you or I have gone,
the wind will rise and cast the moon
as pale reminder above these trees
that it is here the sky abides
and summer still prevails

untitled

quince in the courtyard
and forsythia at the door
tufts of cottonwood, dogwood,
silver-trembling birch -

I can trace a path of trees
all the way from the red maples
of climbing youth
to the scarred cedar in the park
the artists come to paint

I come from ramblings
of green gooseberries,
and deep pools where elusive,
the trout hide beneath the eddies

the shape of that space
is the shape of me -
the dense coils of the ivy
belying the brambles

even then the crows
scolded *go! go! go!*
until I left, carrying the lilacs
tight clustered in my chest

so that home may grow
wherever my feet
might be planted

summer so long ago

along down that path
that wrapped beneath the pines,
the wintergreen crept wild
between the scrub grass
and the ferns

we were young there,
counting the lichens
and discovering that moss
has no real direction

that unmistakable creak of oars
in rusted oarlocks
and the clank of stringers
against the side of the boat
will always be summer

with the reek of dead perch
and leaning dangerously far
over the side of the boat
to snag a water lily

we whooped like Indians
racing our frogs along the shore
until it became too dark
to tell the sky from water
except for the winking stars

the cabin has since gone -
burned to a husk by
the same summer lightning

we used to watch
flash above the lake

it's all so much smaller now
somehow, and summer so long ago

reason for roaming

it's the call of the loon to the one
who makes of her a pair

or the strings of the guitar
in perfectly plucked *arpeggio*
on a farmhouse porch
to an audience of moths

it's the lure of the grasses
bending their way to wider sky
or how the blackbird cocks
his head at a turning in the wind

it's the way the road approaches
a rise like every ascent lifts us
higher than ourselves

this is the reason for roaming -
so that we might be elsewhere
imagining home

the sojourner's tale

truth be told
it's more often
the rivers I dream about
than it is the roads,
and the silences
that bend the reeds
to nodding acceptance
that it will ever be
they who sway
and not the world
beneath them

it's when you step
off the gray roads
and into the sudden cold
of damp grass,
into the songs
of the peepers,
or the prairie sighs
that you feel as if you carry
the wide moon's rising within,
full and impossible
yet true

it is then that sleeping
becomes the reawakening
of mind and feet
and trails of tales
only a sojourner can tell
in passing

it's a crow's life,
a night's embrace,
and all the days
before this one
seem nothing but
the dust-dreams
of mice

birthright

perhaps it's my little toe,
which I suspect is part Romany,
and just might explain the itch
to place equal parts of road
before and behind me

but then again it could be the hair,
which has been accused of wildness,
and which revels (I think)
in the ions of new spaces,
utterly refusing to remain
straight-laced and complacent

I think too, that a rush of swallows
maybe stilled themselves quite suddenly
one thousand miles south the day I was born,
thinking *this one will fly*

I imagine they are there still,
waiting for the day I finally find
my wings and catch them up

plotting the route

it's the curves that call to me
a wandering trail of blue
marked upon the heart's map

whole spans of mountains
reduced to points to bend
our roads around

this abridged landscape
through postage stamp prairies
thin slivers of a gorge
I could leap with my fingers

I have finally traced
my itinerant way home

the cypress

the crows beside
scatter suddenly
to higher branches
in a fury of black
recriminations
while I and the old cypress
hold our silence,
watching how the early sun
shifts and stirs
the shadows on the rise
from gray to green
and back again

there is life in scars
I think,
and in missing limbs -
we could not be we
without that rounded edge
of a long-gone branch,
an absence that breathes -
so I keep my peace
beneath this tree
and reflect
oh, how fiercely
must the winds
have loved us!

lake-hearted

I am lake-hearted
easily stirred
pebbles held deep beneath
with the silver-glinting
memories of fish
caught long summers ago
and released again,
absolved of hooks
but never any wiser
to the lure

birds

home, wherever it is,
will have a porch

- front, back, side,
wrap-around, white-washed,
or simple worn wood -

a place to watch
the birds as they flit
and perch and turn
the earth

it is the birds that are
responsible, you know,
for the world's rotation,
- something the scientists
will never tell you

how would it look
to suddenly turn away
from gravities and orbits,
from physics, and say
look, it's the migration
of the swallows that actually
pulls winter across the sky,
a trail of gray behind them

and it's the returning
of the ducks, without which
there'd be no onslaught of
spring rains, and that green

that seems so immediate
all five senses embrace it -
even the worms
are overwhelmed, and drown
themselves to reach it

in the long-shadowed hours

the day always holds its most intensity
in that final flash of afternoon
as it succumbs to dusk
behind the poplars on the hill

I tuck you beneath work-worn arms,
heart felled like sun-ripe wheat
beneath the sharp arc of a yellow moon

you are ever the trail home through the fields
in the long-shadowed hours -
well-trod, whispering -
and the redeeming cool as sweat dispels,

leaving a layer of the day's dust
and want so thick,
you could draw lines through it
with the tip of a finger

how it is you rise within, lapping at me
as curls of water on damp sand,
tilting the hours away
as stars slide their gaze into blue

but how, I wonder,
does one find rest within a river,
succor within the rush of unquenched drives

I may never learn that truth,
but as long as I have the heft of you
here, at the end of the golden day,
it is enough to carry me through

with the sweet grass

I keep you here
with the sweet grass
and the sage,
in the sweeping slant
of soughing plains,
with the pink winds
and waking golds
of light rising slow
along the river

I keep you here,
and just there,
beyond the tilt
of widening sky,
where sleeping wishes
bending lie
to rest with
dreaming grasses

perception

it's not true, what they say -

the moon you look up at
is not the same moon that I see

mood casts a different hue,
as does latitude,
and whether your hands
are folded, or spread wider
than the distance
between the fireflies

outside Doolin, the moon
is the stone the villagers
tossed up into the sky one night -
to see could they make
the stars rain into their river

which hasn't yet happened,
though the river still anticipated
while we sat and unwrapped
our humble sandwiches beside it

but the January moon
I stood in the cold to watch,
and which rose up from my throat,
is the one I could not find the words
to call back down again

and is the one that rises
still in August, remaining out

of reach in the quivering elm,
while your moon flies much
more distant and illumines
the unbending pine

on the Burren

today
a certain slant of light
sudden and particular
recalled an autumn
plunging eager
among cracked rocks
and impossible wind,
bean sidhe
wild at rest in the crests,
untouching the slight white
- remember - of the flower
that defied the rocks
to bloom impervious

a piece of that place
has settled stalwart,
just here,
unfeasibly flowering
in uncertain light
and Burren stone

migration

how long I sat,
oars stilled,
when the heron
broke the calm
between the reeds -
a grace of gray
among the bending
green

that day I knew
the difference
between solitude
and not having you

later, when the geese
flew over low,
more than air rushed
among that hush
of wings in tandem
flight

their silent arrow
drew me, urgent
and migratory
beyond those grasses
brushed by sky,
and gathered
me home

here now the forsythia
has bloomed yellow

three times upon
the stems outside
my door

and somewhere
near you
a waking laurel
again casts pale
shadows at your feet
and wonders
what it is that
keeps you

leaving Forsyth

5 a.m. just west of Forsyth - it's me, the dog,
and the road rising gray between the plateaus

the night before, I'd met a man from Newark
drinking beer in the rutted lot of a dingy motel

said he'd finally had it - suffocating
under a shroud of smog and metal -
gave everything away but the car
and the clothes he was wearing

and just drove until something about
the luster of the river outside of town
finally stopped him

now, he says, he can breathe -
says he walks that river every morning
and thinks *this* is the more he didn't
know he was looking for

I packed up the car and the dog and drove on
before the sun could pull itself up above the hills

and when I looked back in the mirror, he was there
on the slope above the unbending folds of the river,
and I could see the city flee from him
like smoke from the fire

outside town, there's no one but me on the road
and at this second, I'm just wise enough to know
that even if I'm still ticking away at ninety,

this moon will never again follow me
sinking low and silver on a blooming dawn,
when just around the bend, the river
throws it back again so that the world
shines in at me from all directions

no direction but home

early morning's best

it's then that I can
almost forgive gas station
coffee for being what it is -
bitter, and too hot
for the tongue

for a stretch of about a hundred miles
I came across no one else at all

and this was peace

crossing through the reservation
I envied the half-collapsed husk
of a trailer for its permanent perch
on the bluff over the valley

I could lie there
painted by grass-shadows
and stretch, ceaseless as sky

I have never found that same
sense of being spread in
all directions, like sudden
light over dawn-dark hills

except in driving alone
on a tireless road, without purpose,
heading no direction but home

passing through Paradise Valley

that twist of smoke rising up
from the valley is not mine,
does not lift itself
from any hearth I know,
nor can I claim the cord
of wood that burns to give it height

this is not my folding slope -
my feet cannot call these grasses theirs -
and the moon creeping up over the rise
is not a moon that rises for my eyes

I do not reside in this place,
where the gold of the earth
rises up to scrape the sky
and where the hills thrust
themselves tenaciously upwards
chasing after hearth-smoke

this spin of wind that tugs
upon the hems of the tamaracks
treats me as a stranger
and brushes by, impatient
for the wings of ravens
yet to arrive

though just passing through,
I might pause to watch
the ebbing day tuck itself away
between the trees beyond ridge
that marks the edge
of paradise not mine

on the Skykomish

on cloudy nights too black
to see the river,
I hear it still
deep in discourse
with the trees,
chortling over the stones -
those bits the mountain
let slip ages ago -
they now congregate
in scattered gatherings
feeling the cool lisp
of the current on its way -
water that never stays

come morning, the sky
will clear itself just enough
that I can watch the moon
break herself open
upon the tallest lodgepole,
black fracturing her faded face
as she sinks into day

the spiders will spin
themselves lower
over the water, webs
precarious flourishes
of light reflected -
in this place,
I am the stranger
wondering at the
tongues of birds,

and river words
my ears cannot fathom
and yet the heart
in silence understands

untitled

Gymnopedie on 9 Mile Creek -
Satie always could play night,
plaintive and pausing,
falling between the crickets

I blame you, old friend,
for August nights
spent purposely lost
somewhere west on
County Highway S

in summer we could always
smell the lake on the left
and hear the highway
singing its way west

and only when the sweet
winds through the open windows
had sated us, did we search out
the radio towers and follow
them back toward
more civilized lights

years later and the asphalt
hasn't left me yet -
that rushing hum of the tires
draws me on, alone on the road
with Satie on an empty night

on leaving the highway

so much of this life was woven of wanting the road,
of the hard dark lure of asphalt swaying
its way through the plains

do you know I have seen skies where there was no sky,
where the trees grew so tall, so close, they choked
the blue from sight as if they strove to hide the stars -
to conceal the sun and all its hourly truths
from searching eyes

in such woods I have stood silent with the doe,
picking her way among ferns - each step of hoof
(slow, deliberate), an affirmation
of *yes, I am alive*

I have seen storms take the light and light
break the storm, and inhaled as giddy
as any opium fiend the rush
of burnt ozone exhilaration

I have felt the forest past midnight
and been taken by its darkness
just as I have lain in autumn fields
beneath stars so ablaze with their own brilliance
that even now I feel the need to pinch myself,
say *yes, I am alive*

but it was when I first heard the wind
and had learned enough to heed it
as it called, bending yellow stalks
into the vague shape of my true name

it was when it sang out from the painted rocks
and from deep within the canyons where the sunset
is pulled from the sky to lie at last with earth as one,
and there, in the place where I learned that light and rock
are the truest of lovers, I first touched free

it was there I stopped to walk through the gray sage
far from the highway in that hour when dawn
is first dawn, there where I came upon the silver pull
of the river as it woke and unwove all those dreams
of the unending road, for it was only upon leaving
the highway I finally knew free

standing with the swallows at dusk

the swallows have returned
to the fields at first dusk,
looping the sky to the earth
in nimble arcing plummets

as if they carry the curve
of the earth in the tips
of their wings - in a flurry
of miniscule heartbeats

that thrum as much being
into the shimmering air
as the cicadas of summer
or the peepers in spring

I am an inconsequential pillar,
an obstacle to dart about
beneath the darkening sky
in their tireless wheeling gavotte

early winter landscape

gold grains stir,
their dry dreams rustling
softly beneath the crest
of a red sun rising
over frost-kissed fields
from stillness waking

stalks bent and broken
here, there, here -
mark the path
of night's passing

the pale arc of the moon
quietly slides
into the pink of morning
and ghost fingers of fog
cling to the darkened hollow
between the earth's curves,
chasing a dark-winged bird
into the yawning sky

quietude

this early, before day
has begun to stretch
and the morning still breathes
its misty calm
the grass lies damp
and a chill from the night before
yet settles on the hill

the wood hints of blues
brushed by softest gray
and a drifting warbler flits
from beneath the pale eyes
of the rhododendron
carrying its solitary song
with not a note of loneliness

two dogs in tow
(the sweetest of companions)
I follow the path and inhale the day
beneath trees whose branches
reach out to greet and twine
with their neighbors'
and for a few sweet, brief moments
this is all that the world contains

www.ingramcontent.com/pod-product-compliance
Lightning Source LLC
Chambersburg PA
CBHW071753020426
42331CB00008B/2303